BALTIMORE
GARDEN
QUILT

Barbara M. Burnham

American Quilter's Society
P. O. Box 3290 • Paducah, KY 42002-3290
www.AmericanQuilter.com

Located in Paducah, Kentucky, the American Quilter's Society (AQS) is dedicated to promoting the accomplishments of today's quilters. Through its publications and events, AQS strives to honor today's quiltmakers and their work and to inspire future creativity and innovation in quiltmaking.

EXECUTIVE BOOK EDITOR: ANDI MILAM REYNOLDS
COPY EDITORS: CHRYSTAL ABHALTER AND BARBARA PITMAN
GRAPHIC DESIGN: ELAINE WILSON
COVER DESIGN: MICHAEL BUCKINGHAM
QUILT PHOTOGRAPHY: CHARLES R. LYNCH
HOW-TO PHOTOGRAPHY: CHARLES R. LYNCH, UNLESS OTHERWISE NOTED

Additional copies of this book may be ordered from the American Quilter's Society, PO Box 3290, Paducah, KY 42002-3290, or online at www.AmericanQuilter.com.

Text © 2012, Author, Barbara M. Burnham
Artwork © 2012, American Quilter's Society

LIBRARY OF CONGRESS CATALOGING-IN-PUBLICATION DATA

Burnham, Barbara M.
　Baltimore Garden Quilt / By Barbara M. Burnham.
　　p. cm.
　Includes bibliographical references.
　Summary: "Original quilt in the Baltimore Album style. The piece is initialed 'M.E.C.' and dated 1848. Features 25 garden theme patterns given full-size on a CD"--Provided by publisher.
　ISBN 978-1-60460-022-3
　1. Quilting--Patterns. 2. Album quilts. I. Title.
　TT835.B847 2012
　746.46'041--dc23

　　　　　　　　2011043955

Photo: M.E.C. 1848 – Block E2, detail – Esther's China Asters

Dedication

To Ed, my best friend and husband, for encouraging me to rescue the old quilt, and for his patience while I followed my vision to recreate the new quilt and write this book.

Acknowledgments

Many thanks to:

Mimi Dietrich and Jeana Kimball for encouragement and advice, and for sharing their love of appliqué and Baltimore-style quilts.

All my friends at the Baltimore Appliqué Society for their enthusiasm and for nudging me to get the quilt finished and publish the patterns.

Marty Vint of Dogwood Quilting of Baltimore, Maryland, for skillfully transforming my tracings of antique hand quilting designs with modern longarm quilting.

Andi Reynolds and American Quilter's Society, for making this book possible.

Contents

Photo: M.E.C. REMEMBERED – Block E2, detail – Esther's China Asters

above: *M.E.C. 1848 - Block C5*
(Eliza's Strawflowers)

right: *M.E.C. 1848 quilt*
photo: Barbara M. Burnham

Introduction

My dear husband thought I was crazy to buy this old, worn-out quilt. Condition, however, is not always a collector's criterion. I envisioned this quilt as it must have looked in 1848—fresh—and my dream was to give it a new life now 150 years later. Although restoration was not a practical option for this quilt, reproduction was.

After many hours tracing the designs from the original quilt and counting the numerous tiny petals on some of the flowers, I wondered if I really was crazy. However, with encouragement from my friends at the Baltimore Appliqué Society (as they begged for the patterns), I set about to make the reproduction quilt. There were many challenges, especially the flowers with almost 50 petals (Block B3, Calvin's Trumpet Creeper, for example).

During the process of making the reproduction quilt, I developed some innovative methods for recreating these complex multi-layer flowers. In this book, I will include all the techniques I used, including a quick, template-free method for sewing the double swags that frame the quilt.

(1) Kimball, Jeana, *Red and Green, An Appliqué Tradition*, That Patchwork Place, Inc., 1990.

The Original Quilt

Red-and-green was a favorite color combination of appliqué quiltmakers in the early- to mid-nineteenth century. [1] The M.E.C. 1848 quilt is a particularly fine example, if we can overlook its worn condition. Such densely worked quilting and detailed appliqué were rarely done because they are so labor intensive. Even elaborate appliqué quilts of the day were more often quilted in lines, grids, or simple yet functional designs. The unique designs in appliqué and quilting found on this quilt exemplify a high level of skill and creative ability. Quiltmakers then would not have had the pattern resources we have today.

Block B3 – Calvin's Trumpet Creeper, detail.

Introduction

The M.E.C. 1848 quilt could be considered transitional between the early red-and-green quilts often made in Pennsylvania, New Jersey, and Maryland, and the more colorful Baltimore album quilts made between 1845 and 1860. These quilts were often stitched by more than one person and made as presentation or friendship quilts with signatures and inked sentiments. Another 1840–1850 era quilt pictured in *The Quilt Digest* [2] has Baltimore inked on three blocks. Two of its blocks have very similar designs found on M.E.C. 1848. Minimal quilting is stitched in double-rodded diagonal lines.

The only provenance we have for M.E.C. 1848 is that it came from an estate in Virginia Beach, Virginia. Finding it was a stroke of luck

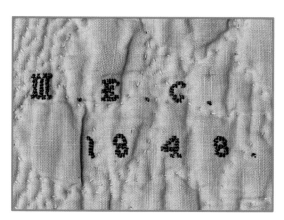

Block C5 – Eliza's Strawflowers, detail.

for me and for preservation of the quilt. (Also, fortunately for me, I found it before my friend, Polly!) I can only hope that the original quiltmaker would have been pleased with the reproduction.

The old quilt's condition is very sad. Much red fabric has gone; the remaining red is very fragile, flaking off at the slightest touch. The background fabric is brittle and has turned to an iced tea color, perhaps due to improper storage. Water stains and paint drippings attest to its long life and will remain forever. One observer's opinion is that the quilt survived a flood; it has evidently endured many events.

Twenty-five 15" x 15" square appliqué blocks are surrounded by a double swag border linked with floral motifs. Among the appliqués, a variety of quilting motifs are emphasized by expert quilting at 9–10 tiny stitches to the inch, in very close lines sewn diagonally across the surface of the quilt.

"M.E.C. 1848" is cross-stitched in the wreath in Block C5 (Eliza's Strawflowers), each tiny stitch crossing only two threads of fabric. Was this the inscription of a talented needlewoman, or an honored recipient? We will never know. Three blocks once had inked signatures, which, sadly, disintegrated the cloth where they were written. Only the edges are left behind to tease our imagination about the signers and the provenance of the quilt.

(2) *The Quilt Digest*, Kiracofe and Kile, 1983, page 36: The quilt pictured has two blocks (A2, D4) similar to the M.E.C. quilt. Swags and birds in block A2 are almost identical, even the vine placed in front of one bird and behind the other. Block D4 has a similar cornucopia and vine. This 1840–1850 quilt includes: "indistinguishable names and dates, and 'Baltimore' appears on three blocks in ink. A fourth block is signed 'Annabele A. Wade'."

M.E.C.
1848.

M.E.C. Remembered - Block C5

(Eliza's Strawflowers)

Introduction

Tracing Designs from the Antique Quilt

To capture the antique designs, I used clear, 12-gauge upholstery vinyl in a method recommended by Pepper Cory. It is easier to see through than tracing paper, and offers less chance of being poked through with a drawing tool.[3]

I cut the vinyl into squares large enough to cover one block with plenty of overlap. Leftover pieces were enough to trace border flowers, a set of double swags, and corner swags. At each corner of the vinyl square, a weight kept the vinyl in place—pins would have left holes, risking damage to the quilt. To trace onto the vinyl, I used a Sharpie® Fine Point permanent marking pen and capped the pen when not in use.

> *Note:* The vinyl is packaged in green tissue paper. Tracings must be stored flat with tissue paper in between to separate them because they can stick together, and ink from one tracing can transfer onto others.

One block at a time, I first drew block seam lines, then carefully traced designs from the quilt—solid lines for appliqué, dotted lines for quilting motifs. This is how the patterns on the CD appear, also. The old quilt was not square, not a single block was straight, and the border swags varied in size and shape. Corner swags were actually gathered to make them fit. Tracings on vinyl were then photocopied onto paper for adjustments—lots of adjustments—before sewing could begin.

The patterns for the new quilt have none of these problems! Everything is straight, square, and sized appropriately.

The Reproduction Quilt— M.E.C. Remembered

A few of the blocks I modified so that none of their designs are lost in the seams, as they almost were on the original. Vines and baskets I made more symmetrical or graceful. Areas of fabric loss and deterioration required some guesswork. Thankfully, missing embroidery stitches left tiny holes to reveal the designs. Some flowers I redesigned slightly, and Block B5 I chose to rotate 45 degrees. Border swags I redrafted into nine equal repeats for each border, with corner swags extending across the border seams.

> *Note:* Block B5 pattern is not rotated.

(3) Cory, Pepper, *Mastering Quilt Marking*, C&T Publishing, 1999, p. 53-54.

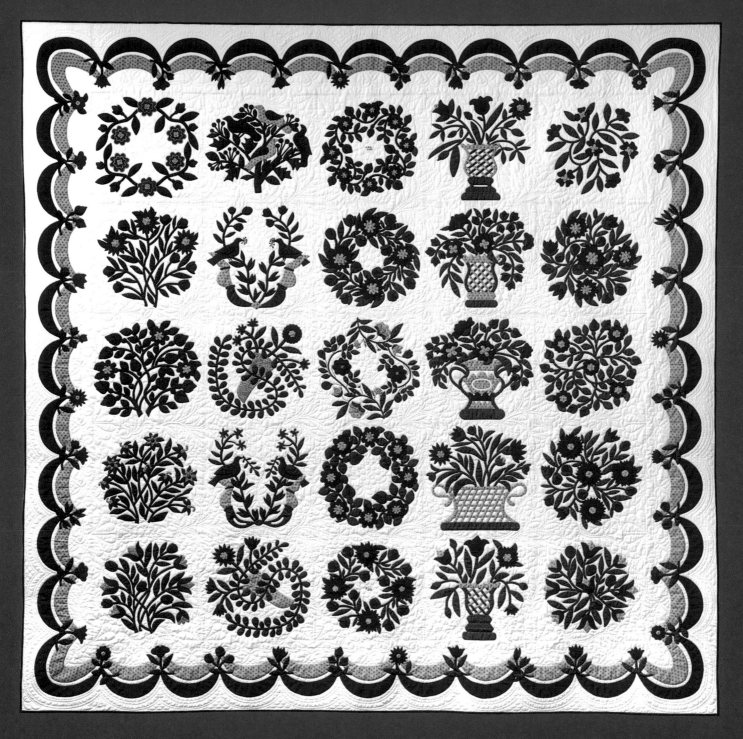

M.E.C. Remembered (91" x 91")

The Reproduction Quilt, made by the author

Introduction

To give fanciful names to each block, I tried to imagine flowers that might have been growing in a Baltimore garden of the 1840s and the ladies and gentlemen who might have cultivated them. See figure 4-1 on page 51 to view the block names.[4]

Looking closely at some of the original red flowers on the quilt, you might see that they are fashioned with many, tiny, single petals, arranged and stitched one at a time. On one flower (Block B3, Calvin's Trumpet Creeper), I counted 48 little ¼" diameter circular petals! Imagine a patient lady in 1848 coaxing each tiny circle into place with her needle and thread by the light of a gas lamp or candle.

Block B3 – Calvin's Trumpet Creeper, details. Top photo from old quilt, bottom photo from reproduction quilt.

While making the reproduction, I devised a method to make these flowers easier to arrange, although my flowers look more uniform than the originals. After struggling with a compass, protractor, circle templates, plastic templates, LOTS of graph paper, and many erasers, I worked the petals into layers which can be rotated and overlapped, yet still give the final impression of single petals. With this method, you can assemble a flower in eight layered pieces, instead of the original 48 tiny pieces. When the same color fabric is used, nobody can tell that these are not 48 separate petals!

Try the technique in Multilayer Flowers on page 33 for a small border flower. Or, for the truly adventurous, try stitching one separate petal at a time as on the original quilt, but please, not by candlelight.

(4) Susan Curtis wrote in *A Flowering of Quilts* edited by Patricia Cox Crews, University of Nebraska Press, 2001, p.12:

"The importation of South American and Mexican "tropical plants", such as nasturtiums and zinnias, in mid-century created a taste for brilliantly colored, exotic flower beds. ... cockscomb, impatiens, and four-o'clocks filled flower beds with their vibrant colors.

"In addition to annuals, gardeners planted bulbs and tuberous flowers in masses. Tulips and narcissus quickly became popular items of commerce in American garden nurseries....

"Dahlias, another flower imported from Mexico, became the rage for nineteenth-century gardeners. By the middle of the century, garden catalogs devoted more space to varieties of dahlias than to any other species. Dahlias remained the most popular flower for massing in beds throughout the second half of the century. And as exotic flowers became popular in garden beds, they also began to appear in the quilts of the time."

Choosing Fabrics

For my quilt, I chose one green and two yellow reproduction fabrics from Judie Rothermel's "Baltimore Album" fabric line by Marcus Brothers, plus a solid Turkey red. Fabric dyed this bright, rich, solid red became very popular with quilters in the mid-1800s because it did not fade or bleed.

To shop for Turkey red fabric today, a skein of embroidery floss is a convenient and portable matching tool. Antique Turkey red fabric matches DMC® Embroidery Floss #304, also a favorite for redwork embroidery.

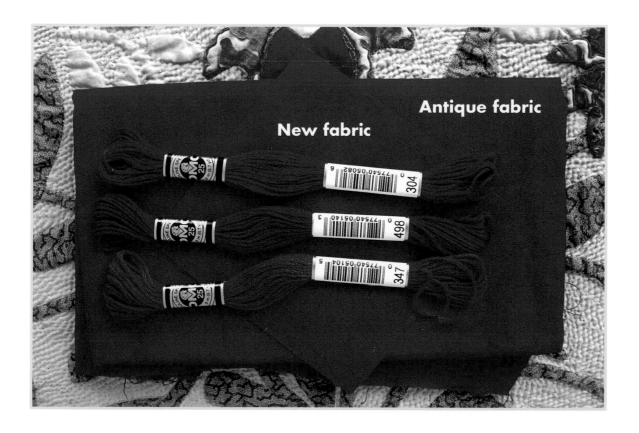

Introduction

Yardage requirements are provided for the whole quilt as I made it, as well as per block (see chart on pages 16–21). Of course, amounts may vary depending on your fabric choices or sewing methods, how many blocks you make and their sizes, and whether you adjust the border measurements I've given.

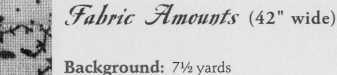

Fabric Amounts (42" wide)

Background: 7½ yards
Choose an off-white or antique white color. See cutting diagrams on page 15. Borders are not mitered.

Green print: 7½ yards
Plan to cut the longest bias stems first. Bias stems alone will require approximately 4 yards.

Red solid: 6 yards
(includes 1¼ yards for binding)
Border swags: 4 strips 6" x 76" long
Corner swags: 4 squares 10" x 10"
Bias binding: approximately 1¼ yards

Yellow print: 2½ yards
Border swags: 4 strips 6" x 76" long
Corner swags: 4 squares 10" x 10"

Backing: 3 yards x 108" wide, or 6 yards if pieced. Make it 4"–6" larger than the top.

Batting: Size of finished quilt plus 2" all around. Choose thin cotton batting to create the feel of an antique quilt.

Binding: See red solid above.

Supply List

Basic Appliqué Supplies

- ❀ Appliqué needles: sharps, straws, or milliner's (I prefer sharps, size 12)
- ❀ Thimble
- ❀ Fabric scissors: sharp, pointed scissors that cut all the way to the point
- ❀ Threads to match appliqué motifs
- ❀ Embroidery floss (6-strand) for blanket stitch and embellishments: green, yellow, brown, red
- ❀ Bits of cotton stuffing or batting for flower centers
- ❀ Bias bars: ⅛", ¼", ⅜", ½"

Supplies for Freezer Paper Appliqué and Block Preparation

- ❀ White ³⁄₁₆" foamcore board, cut to at least 16" x 16"
- ❀ Dritz® Ball Point Pins Multi Color 1¹⁄₁₆" (not the long quilter's pins)
- ❀ Freezer paper
- ❀ Paper or craft scissors: pointed, for accurate cutting of freezer paper
- ❀ Mechanical pencil (fine point 0.5 mm)
- ❀ Neutral 50-wt. sewing thread for basting
- ❀ Basting needle: darner or embroidery sharp
- ❀ Iron (no steam), a flat ironing surface, and terrycloth towel
- ❀ Tweezers
- ❀ Circle template for various size circles

❀ Manila folder

❀ Original pattern, plus pattern photo-copy (or print original twice). Photocopy the pattern or print two copies, because pin basting will leave pinholes in your pattern.

❀ Number the motifs on your pattern with pencil, to reference placement.

Supplies for Blanket Stitch with Fusible

❀ Paper-backed, lightweight, iron-on fusible adhesive such as HeatnBond® Lite made by Therm O Web, or similar product

Supplies for Hand Quilting and Finishing

❀ Marker of your choice. Always test them to make sure marks will come out after quilting.

❀ Light source or light box

❀ Basting needle: darner or embroidery sharp

❀ White thread for basting

❀ Hand quilting needles: I prefer size 12 betweens

❀ Hand quilting thread to match background fabric

❀ Thimble

Cutting Diagrams

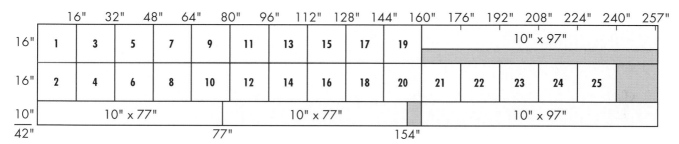

Blocks and border fabric

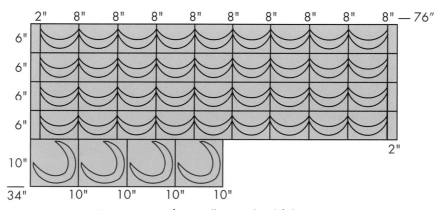

Swags — cut from yellow and red fabrics

Introduction

Use this chart to plan single blocks

FABRIC REQUIREMENTS		
Block No.	**Red**	**Yellow**
A1	14" x 14"	6" x 6"
A2	12" x 12"	6" x 6"
A3	12" x 12"	4" x 4"
A4	10" x 10"	6" x 6"
A5	8" x 8"	5" x 5"
B1	8" x 8" (cherries)	7" x 7" (birds)
	7" x 7" (birds)	
B2	9" x 9"	7" x 7"
B3	10" x 10" (leaves)	7" x 7"
	9" x 9" (big flower)	
B4	9" x 9"	7" x 7"
B5	10" x 10" (leaves)	7" x 7"
	9" x 9" (big flower)	
C1	17" x 17"	5" x 5"
C2	15" x 15"	5" x 5"
C3	7" x 7"	7" x 7" (or two different yellows)
C4	17" x 17"	6" x 6"
C5	17" x 17"	8" x 8"

Block No.	Green	Green Bias Strips ONLY
A1	10" x 10"	½" wide – 40" (12" x 12")
		¼" wide – 8" (13" x 13")
A2	14" x 14"	¼" wide – 80" (12" x 12")
A3	15" x 15"	¼" wide – 80" (12" x 12")
A4	14" x 14"	¼" wide – 80" (12" x 12")
A5	12" x 12"	¼" wide – 60" (12" x 12")
B1	14" x 14" (incl. cut stem shapes)	⅛" wide – 40" (cherry stems) (9" x 9")
B2	11" x 11"	¼" wide – 40" (10" x 10")
		⅛" wide – 6" (14" x 14")
B3	12" x 12"	⅜" wide – 10" (flower stems)
		¼" wide – 37" continuous piece
		¼" wide – 8" (flower stems) (30" x 30")
B4	12" x 12"	¼" wide – 40" (11" x 11")
		⅛" wide – 8" (flower stems) (14" x 14")
B5	12" x 12"	¼" wide – 10" (flower stems)
		¼" wide – 37" (continuous piece)
		¼" wide – 6" (flower stems) (30" x 30")
C1	13" x 13"	¼" wide – 50" (12" x 12")
C2	15" x 15"	¼" wide – 40" (12" x 12")
C3	15" x 15"	⅛" wide – 36" (10" x 10")
C4	14" x 14"	¼" wide – 36" (12" x 12")
C5	14" x 14"	¼" wide – 40" (12" x 12")

Block No.	Red	Yellow
D1	9" x 9"	6" x 6" square (incl. basket top, sides)
WEAVERS See page 46		26" total length (6" x 6")
D2	12" x 12"	6" x 6" square
WEAVERS See page 46		25" total length (6" x 6")
D3	10" x 10"	8" x 8"
D4	9" x 9"	10" x 10" (cut shapes for basket top & sides)
WEAVERS See page 46		88" total length (9" x 15")
D5	9" x 9"	6" x 6" for basket
WEAVERS See page 46		20" total length (6" x 6")
E1	10" x 10"	5" x 5"
E2	16" x 16"	5" x 5"
E3	14" x 14"	8" x 8"
E4	20" x 20"	5" x 5"
E5	10" x 10"	6" x 6"

FABRIC REQUIREMENTS (continued)

Block No.	Green	Green Bias Strips ONLY
D1	12" x 12"	¼" wide BIAS for stems – 40"
WEAVERS on straight grain	¼" wide strips on STRAIGHT GRAIN for basket weavers — 25" total length (6" x 6")	⅛" wide – 6" (12" x 12")
D2	14" x 14" (incl. cut shapes for basket sides)	¼" wide – 35" BIAS for stems (12" x 12")
WEAVERS on straight grain	¼" wide strips on STRAIGHT GRAIN for basket weavers — 25" total length (6" x 6")	
D3	15" x 15" (cut shapes for basket sides)	¼" wide – 32" (10" x 10")
D4	14" x 14"	¼" wide – 48" (12" x 12")
WEAVERS on straight grain		
D5	13" x 13"	¼" wide – 40" (12" x 12")
WEAVERS on straight grain	¼" wide on STRAIGHT GRAIN for basket weavers 20" total length (6" x 6")	
E1	11" x 11"	¼" wide – 40" (10" x 10")
E2	14" x 14"	¼" wide – 48" (13" x 13")
E3	15" x 15"	¼" wide – 65" (15" x 15")
E4	15" x 15"	¼" wide – 50" (15" x 15")
E5	12" x 12"	¼" wide – 40" (11" x 11")

FABRIC REQUIREMENTS (continued)		
Block No.	**Red**	**Yellow**
Border Swags Need 76" continuous	(continuous cut 6" x 76") (x 4 borders)	(continuous cut 6" x 76"*) (x 4 borders)
Corner Swags	10" x 10" (cut 4)	10" x 10" (cut 4)
Border Flowers	5" x 5" for simple flower	Scraps
	7" x 7" for multilayer flowers	
=====	=====	=====
Bias Binding	Cut 2" wide to make ⅜" finished – (36" x 36")	

Background Fabric (42" wide)		
See cutting diagram on page 15		
	Cut Size	**Finished Size**
Blocks	16" x 16"	15" x 15"
Top & Bottom Borders	10" x 77"	8" x 75"
2 Side Borders	10" x 97"	8" x 95"
Total – 7¼ yards minimum		

Block No.	Green	Green Bias Strips ONLY
Border Swags Need 76" continuous		
Corner Swags		
Border Flowers	2" x 2" (x 144 leaves)	Each stem requires approx. 5" length of ¼" wide bias strip (x 40 flowers) (16" x 16")
=====	=====	===
Bias Binding		
Total green	7½ yards	

M.E.C. Remembered - Block BI
(George's Cherry Tree)

General Instructions

Background Preparation

Wash all fabrics first in warm water with mild detergent, as the finished quilt will be.

From the background fabric, plan to cut borders first, then blocks. Cut blocks and borders 1"–2" too large all around because sometimes appliqué shrinks a block or edges fray. It is easy to trim edges later, but impossible to add more.

On each block, pencil mark a T at the top center edge along the crosswise grain. This will help to keep all blocks on the same grain, and prevent confusion with alignments on symmetrical blocks, such as wreath designs.

Hint: Crosswise grain refers to the threads that run perpendicular to the selvage. These are the threads that can be easily pulled along the cut edge of the fabric as it comes off the bolt. Lengthwise grain refers to the threads that run the length of the fabric, parallel to the selvage. Bias grain lies at right angles to the lengthwise and crosswise grain of the fabric. Bias has more stretch than straight or crosswise grain.

Appliqué with Freezer Paper on Top

There are many methods of appliqué, both by hand and machine, and I enjoy them all! Use your preferred methods, and expand your appliqué toolbox with several techniques on this quilt. My favorite method uses freezer paper on top as a guide for stitching.

1. Get organized

Number the motifs on your pattern. (No need to number stems.) These numbers will guide appliqué placement on the block, like a numbered jigsaw puzzle.

2. Trace freezer paper templates

Freezer paper has a dull side (for tracing) and a shiny plastic side (for ironing to appliqué fabric). With a sharp pencil (a mechanical pencil will keep a thin, sharp point), trace the birds, leaves, flowers, etc., onto the paper's dull side. As you trace each motif, include those jigsaw numbers from your pattern.

You could trace the whole block as one unit, but to maximize freezer paper, motifs can be traced one at a time, in any direction, close

General Instructions

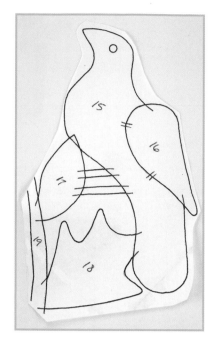

Fig. 2–1

together. Some motifs can be traced as one unit, such as the bird and its wing. As you trace, extend lines slightly into adjoining parts. Add double hash marks to cross the line dividing the bird and wing (Fig. 2–1). The extensions and hash marks will be cut apart when you cut out the bird and wing templates, and each will be pressed onto different fabrics. When you arrange the fabric pieces on your block, those added marks on the templates can be reunited to help with alignments.

For multilayer flowers, templates are drawn in overlapping sections (see Multilayer Flowers on pages 33–39).

Templates are not needed for basket weaves or stems. Basket weaves are made with straight grain strips called "weavers" in the Fabric Requirements chart on pages 16–21; also see Woven Baskets on page 46. Graceful, curved stems can be made with lengths of bias tubes (see Bias Stems on pages 45–46).

3. Cut out templates

With small paper scissors, cut out the freezer paper motifs on the pencil-drawn lines.

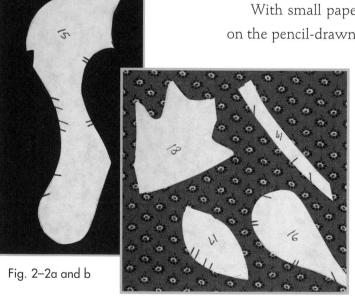

Fig. 2–2a and b

4. Press templates to fabric front

Arrange each freezer paper piece (shiny side down) onto the front of the appliqué fabric. Leave enough space between each piece to allow at least ³⁄₁₆" seam allowance all around every piece when the fabric is cut apart (Fig. 2–2a and b).

Press motifs to fabrics with a warm, dry iron. The shiny side of the freezer paper will stick to the fabric.

BALTIMORE GARDEN QUILT ❁ *Barbara M. Burnham*

Hint: If you discover later while stitching that your freezer paper comes loose, your iron was not warm enough. Simply press again with a warmer iron. However, if your iron is too hot, the freezer paper will be difficult to remove and could leave excess residue behind, so experiment with your iron.

5. Cut out fabric motifs

Cut out the fabric motifs, adding a ³⁄₁₆" seam allowance outside the freezer paper edge (estimate halfway between ⅛"–¼"). Leave the paper on. Store the pieces for each block in a reclosable plastic bag until needed. Label the block number on the bag.

No-mark Method of Appliqué Placement

A small block is shown here. The method is the same for any block or border.

1. Align pattern and background fabric

Begin with a white foamcore board as a base to work on. On top of it place a copy of the paper pattern. Keep the original pattern handy for visual reference.

Lightly fold the background fabric in quarters and gently crease with your fingers to mark the block center and edge centers. Lay the background fabric on top of the pattern copy, matching center and side points. You should be able to see through the fabric slightly to the pattern underneath.

Secure these three layers by sticking a few ballpoint pins straight down through the background fabric and the paper pattern into the foamcore board (Fig. 2–3).

Fig. 2–3

2. Place and pin appliqué motifs

Begin by placing the leaves first. Looking through the background fabric to the pattern underneath, align each leaf into position. Stick a ballpoint pin straight down through the leaf and the pattern into the foamcore board to hold the motif in place. Do not go through the back of the foamcore. Add two or three more pins so the piece does not slide around.

Wherever pieces will overlap, place only the bottom one. After the bottom motifs are

General Instructions

appliquéd, the upper pieces are placed as needed. With practice, it is possible to appliqué with multiple overlapping pieces basted in place.

3. Baste appliqué motifs to background

Baste the pinned appliqué pieces to the background fabric, one at a time. Start from the outermost pieces and work toward the center. After a few basting stitches, pull out any pins no longer needed. Be careful not to stitch through the paper pattern underneath. Keep knots on the top of the appliqué pieces, so the basting threads are easy to remove later (Fig. 2–4).

Realign the block onto the pattern and pin it into place to baste more pieces.

For stems, begin at the top end and arrange a bias stem onto the background fabric. Be sure enough of the cut end of the stem will lie underneath the flower so the flower can hide that raw edge. Stick one pin straight down into the bias stem and into the pattern and foamcore. Continue to align the stem in place, sticking pins through and working toward the other end of the stem. Adjust as needed to form a graceful curve, making sure the stem covers the raw edges of the leaves. Cut off any extra length (Fig. 2–5).

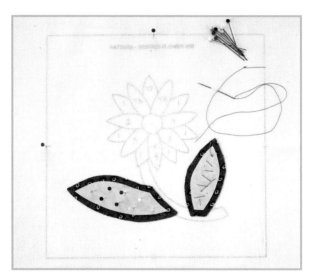

Fig. 2–4

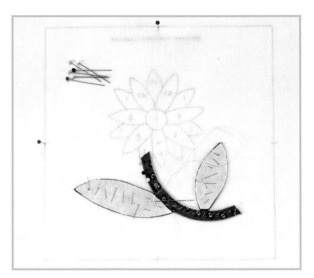

Fig. 2–5

4. Appliqué motifs to background

When basting is complete and pins are removed, lift the block up away from the pattern and appliqué around the edges of the leaves. Where leaves lie along the stem, leave the seam allowance flat (unturned), because the stem will cover that edge.

Appliqué the stem on one side from top to bottom, turn under and appliqué the bottom end, and continue to appliqué the other side. The top end should be left raw (not appliquéd) where it will lie under the flower.

Hand Appliqué with Blind Stitch

The Appliqué Stitch

Use a long, sharp needle designed for appliqué. Choose thread to match the appliqué piece, not the background fabric. Cut a length of thread about 15"–18" long (about from the needle to your elbow), and knot the thread at one end.

The best place to begin appliquéing is along a straight area, such as the middle of the long edge of a leaf, not near points or tight curves. However, if part of the leaf will be covered over later, begin at that point, leaving the seam allowance flat (unturned) where overlapping motifs will hide that edge.

Begin by inserting the needle under the seam allowance of the appliqué piece, right at the stitching line (at the edge of the freezer paper). Pull the thread through so that the knot lies directly under the fabric of the appliqué piece. Knots and thread tails hidden underneath the appliqué will never appear at the back of the block or show through the background (Fig. 2–6).

The following assumes you are a right-handed stitcher. Hold the block loosely gathered in your left hand, thumb on top of the leaf, and other fingers holding underneath.

Use the pointed edge of the needle to push the seam allowance under. The edge of the freezer paper is your turning guide. Leave only the tiniest bit of appliqué fabric (a thread or two) showing along the freezer paper edge, just enough to pierce with a needle. Proceed to turn the seam allowance under for about 1" from your starting point. Use your needle to smooth the seam allowance, sliding under it to even out any bumps. Hold this "turn under" flat against the background fabric using your left thumb and finger.

Take the first appliqué stitch by inserting the needle into the background fabric at the same point where the knot is hiding in the appliqué piece).

Tilt the point of the needle parallel to the drawn line of the appliqué piece. Travel only a tiny distance, about 1/16"–1/8", along the back of the block. For a right-handed stitcher, this

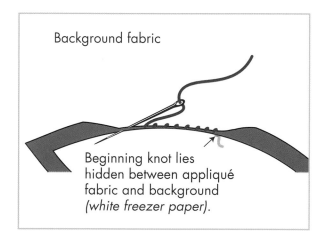

Background fabric

Beginning knot lies hidden between appliqué fabric and background *(white freezer paper).*

Fig. 2–6

General Instructions

would be right-to-left. (With some experience, you can stitch in either direction—just turn the block around!) Bring the needle back up through the background fabric and through the folded seam allowance edge of the appliqué piece. Catch only a few threads of the appliqué edge. After pulling this first stitch snug, the appliqué piece begins to lie flat.

Exactly where this stitch came up, jump right off the edge and insert the needle back into the background fabric. If you move too far away from the edge, your stitches will show.

Continue appliquéing, pulling each stitch snug before beginning the next, one stitch at a time. Keep turning the seam allowance under a little at a time, just enough to hold with your left thumb and finger, smoothing with your needle as you go.

Hint: If your stitches are too tight, the appliqué will ripple; too loose, and the appliqué might not lie flat and smooth. If your appliqué stitches are too far apart (too long), the motifs could lift away from the background when quilted. Frays could occur at inner and outer points. Curved edges could appear bumpy instead of smoothly curved. Conclusion: Closer stitches make smoother curves.

Hint: If you leave just a hair's width of seam allowance showing beyond the edge of the freezer paper, you will be able to stitch without piercing the paper. (It's OK to pierce the paper, but when you remove it later, your stitches might be pulled loose and are more likely to show.)

Concave and Convex Curves

When stitching concave curves (inside a U-shape), clip into the seam allowance along the curve, so that after turning under it will spread apart slightly and lie flat inside the shape. Do not clip all the way to the freezer paper edge, or the fabric could fray. Leave at least a thread or two of fabric unclipped. Never clip out notches; make only straight clips perpendicular to the curve (Fig. 2–7).

Do not clip convex curves. If an appliquéd curve seems bumpy, you can usually improve it by sliding the point of the needle under the appliqué to work out bumps in the seam allowance, or push the bumps in with the point

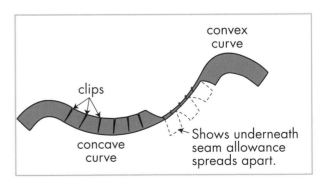

Fig. 2–7

of the needle and squeeze between your thumb and finger. A narrow seam allowance will help you make curves smoother. When curves are very acute, such as around a circle, smaller stitches closer together will help keep the curve smooth (Fig. 2–7, page 28).

Inner Points

When you reach an inner point (like the V at the top of a heart), use small, sharp scissors to clip into the seam allowance straight into the V point. Hold the scissors perpendicular to the point. Do not clip all the way into the freezer paper, but leave a hair's width uncut. Turn under the seam allowance as you approach the V point and stitch all the way up to the point. Take one stitch right into the V point, biting just a bit more seam allowance than usual, even piercing the freezer paper if necessary. This will prevent little frays from poking out later. If there is a fray, use the side of the needle to gently sweep it back under before taking the next stitch to secure the fray. Then turn under the seam allowance on the other side of the V and continue stitching.

Outer Points

When you reach an outer point, such as the bottom point of a heart, do not clip off the seam allowance. Keep turning the seam allowance and stitching along the first edge, all the way to the tip of the point. Make the last stitch at the pointed edge of the freezer paper. Insert the needle into the background fabric right at the

end of the point. Bring the needle up from the back into the appliqué piece between the last two stitches. (The previous stitch at the point will now be secure and cannot wobble or pull out.) Complete the stitch by returning the needle to the back of the block. This stitch prevents seam allowance frays from poking out later.

If this is a very sharp (acute) point, you can now carefully trim out some of the bulk from under the appliqué piece near the point. Small, sharp-pointed scissors are best for this. Leaving the block flat, slip the point of the scissors under the appliqué point, perpendicular, to trim some of the seam allowance that is already stitched down. The unstitched side may be trimmed so that the seam allowance is slightly smaller nearest the point. However, trimming too much will make the next step very difficult.

Using the tip of the needle, but not piercing the point, carefully turn the point under, dragging it with the needle tip. Before extracting the needle, squeeze the point between thumb and finger. This finger pressing will help to keep the seam allowance from popping out, and seems to give the fabric a bit of memory (Fig. 2–8, page 30).

Keeping your thumb and finger squeezed at the point, roll your thumb slightly out of the way, and continue to turn the opposite seam allowance. Bring the needle up through the background and through the seam allowance near the point, and continue to appliqué the piece.

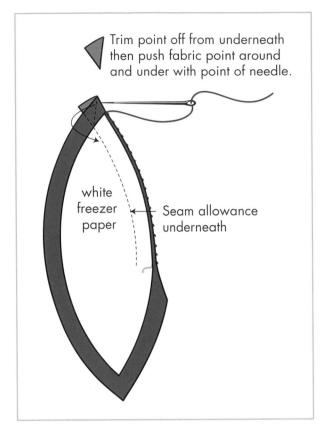

Trim point off from underneath then push fabric point around and under with point of needle.

white freezer paper

Seam allowance underneath

Fig. 2–8

Ending the Appliqué Thread

When the thread becomes short or the appliqué motif is complete, end the thread on the back of the block. Working from the back of the block near where the needle last emerged, take one tiny stitch behind the appliqué piece, catching only the background fabric. Before pulling the thread tight, pass the needle under the thread loop. Do this again on top of that stitch (or nearby) to secure the thread.

Before clipping off waste thread, hide the thread end. (When your quilt is finished and quilted, colored threads hanging loose might shadow through, detracting from your beautiful appliqué.) Near the ending knot on the back of the work and within the stitching lines of the appliqué motif, pierce the background fabric. Run the needle between the background and the appliqué motif, coming out of the background fabric about a needle's length away. Pull this all the way through and clip the remaining thread near the background fabric. This will keep your work secure and neat, and no loose threads will be left to snag or show.

Pressing Appliqué

Press the appliqué face down into a fluffy terrycloth towel. Terrycloth allows the appliqué (especially multilayer appliqué) to sink into the towel, yet gives the background enough support to be pressed smooth. Never press finished appliqué from the front; it can cause the appliqué to flatten, seam allowances to show or become shiny, and cause the background to rumple.

Trimming Blocks

After the appliqué blocks are completed, trim away the edges to square them off. Remember to keep a ¼" seam allowance all around for joining the blocks and borders. Some beautiful antique quilt blocks survive alone in a drawer because that important detail was overlooked.

M.E.C. Remembered - Block A2

(Mary Ann's Mum Garden)

Additional Techniques

How to Make Circles for Berries

1. Use a plastic circle template to draw accurate circles. On a manila folder, draw a circle the desired finished size of the circle. Cut out the circle for a template (Fig. 3–1).

2. On the back of your fabric draw the same circle surrounded by a ½" seam allowance. For example, a ½" circle requires a 1" diameter circle for seam allowance; a ¾" circle requires 1¼" for seam allowance. Cut out the fabric along the larger circle (Fig. 3–2).

3. With strong quilting thread, run a gathering stitch all around between the inner circle and the cut edge. Start and stop on the fabric front and leave both long ends of thread hanging loose (Fig. 3–2).

4. Tie the gathering threads loosely once, and place the manila folder template in the center of the fabric circle. Pull the tie to gather the fabric tightly around the template. Hold the tie with one finger and knot the thread again tightly to secure the gathers. Leave the long ends of thread hanging loose (Fig. 3–2).

5. Press the circle with a hot iron and let it cool. Snip the gathering thread and pull those threads out (Fig. 3–3).

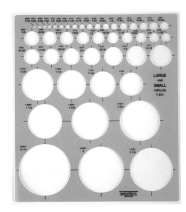

Fig. 3–1. Circle Template

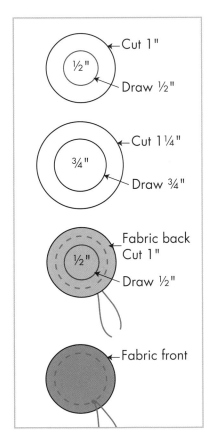

Fig. 3–2. Making circles for berries

6. Remove the template and slip a bit of cotton batting inside. The stuffing adds dimension and softens the effect of the gathering that lies underneath (Fig. 3–3).

7. Place and appliqué the circle berry to the block.

Multilayer Flowers

Once you understand the concept of how to make this flower, you can apply the same technique to other flowers in the quilt, although the number and shape of the petals will vary.

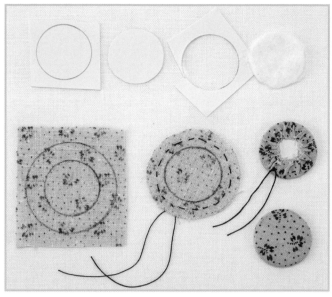

Fig. 3–3. Circle berries or flower centers

Sample Project: Border Flower T5

The following example shows step-by-step how to complete a multilayer border flower with three layers plus one single petal and a circle. You could use this border flower, which is shown on the border layout (see page 51), or any border flower on your quilt's name label.

Solid or almost solid colors (tone-on-tone) work best for multilayered flowers because the slight elevation of the seam allowance visually outlines the petals. With each

Additional Techniques

layer, the flower becomes more dimensional. Busy prints make the individual petals visually disappear into a jumble.

For this border flower you will need:

* Basic appliqué supplies (page 14)
* Pattern and pattern copy (see CD)
* Fabrics:
  * 7½" square background
  * 6" square of red for flower
  * Scraps of green for leaves and a 4" x 1" bias strip for stem
  * Scrap of yellow for flower center
* 1 small circle of batting

1. Appliqué leaves and stems first following General Instructions (pages 23–30). Set aside.

2. On one pattern, in pencil, number each petal by layer. Draw a center dot for layer alignments, and choose one petal to serve as "T" for top. Make separate freezer paper templates for each layer, as explained below. As each layer is appliquéd, it serves as a base to align the next layer.

Trace each layer separately. Try to be as accurate as possible. Use pencil so you can erase if needed. I used ink and heavy pencil for illustration purposes only (Fig. 3–4).

Flower layer 1:

* Mark the center dot and center circle. **IMPORTANT!** The center dot is needed for all layers.

* Mark a T for top alignment and label this layer number "1."

* Trace a solid line at the outer edges of layer 1 petals. The solid lines indicate appliqué stitching lines (A).

* Draw alignment marks at each neighboring petal (B). (These marks will help to guide your placement of the NEXT layer, after layer 1 is appliquéd.)

* Draw a dotted line below where the petals of the next layer will overlap. Because upper petals will cover the space between these petals, it is not necessary to appliqué along dotted lines (C). The dotted line indicates the cutting line for the freezer paper template (Fig. 3–4).

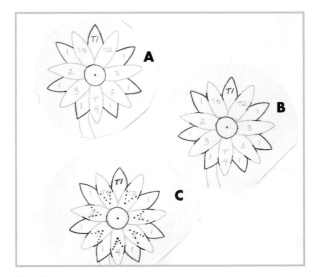

Fig. 3–4

Flower layer 2:

Follow the same steps as layer 1, adding alignment marks for neighboring petals.

- ❀ Mark the center dot.

- ❀ Mark a T for top alignment and label the layer number 2.

- ❀ Trace a solid line at the outer edges of layer 2 petals to indicate appliqué stitching lines, ending at the center circle.

- ❀ Add alignment marks on neighboring petals to guide placements of layers 1 and 3.

- ❀ Draw a dotted line below where petals of the next layer will overlap to indicate the cutting line for the freezer paper template.

Flower layer 3:

Follow the same steps as layer 2, adding alignment marks and T3.

Flower layer 4:

Layer 4 is a single petal. Trace the petal with solid lines for appliqué stitching. Add a dotted line around the top to include the center dot for alignment (Fig. 3–5).

3. Carefully cut out each freezer paper template in one piece along the solid and dotted lines.

4. Arrange the templates, shiny side down, onto the right side of the appliqué fabrics, spacing them far enough apart that every piece will have at least ³⁄₁₆" seam allowance all around it. With a warm iron, press them to the appliqué fabric (Fig. 3–6).

Fig. 3–5

Fig. 3–6

Fig. 3–7

Fig. 3–8

Fig. 3–9

5. Cut out each fabric piece adding ³⁄₁₆" seam allowance outside the freezer paper edge.

6. Baste and appliqué layer 1.

❀ Lay the pattern facing up on the foam-core.

❀ Lay the background fabric with the ap-pliquéd leaves and stem centered over the pattern. Secure them both to the foamcore by inserting at least two ball-point pins.

❀ Pick up the layer 1 piece. Place the piece on the foamcore anywhere and stick a ballpoint pin right through its center dot.

❀ Lift layer 1 and its center pin in your hand. Look through the background fabric to the pattern below. Stick the pin straight down at the center dot on the pattern into the foamcore. Lift a petal or two and peek underneath to check alignment (Fig. 3–7).

❀ Spin the piece into its correct position. Align the T1 on the freezer paper with the T1 on the pattern; use all the marks to guide alignment.

❀ Stick in a few more pins to stabilize lay-er 1 (Fig. 3–8).

❀ Baste layer 1, removing pins as needed. Do not sew into the paper pattern un-derneath (Fig. 3–9).

✿ With thread to match the flower fabric, appliqué along the solid lines at the freezer paper edge around each petal. Clip straight into the V between each petal. At each dotted line, take a long stitch underneath between petals, skipping over to appliqué the next petal. There is no need to appliqué the Vs between petals because the next layer will cover them (Figs. 3–10a and b).

✿ When all the petals of layer 1 are appliquéd, remove the basting stitches, but leave the freezer paper on to guide alignment of the next layer.

Fig. 3–10a

7. Baste and appliqué layer 2.

✿ Refer to the pattern for alignment of T2. Align this layer just like layer 1. Spin the new layer into its position. Match up the petal marked T2 and match up alignment marks on the previous layer's freezer paper template. At this point, you might be able to estimate placement, sliding the template evenly between neighboring petals (Fig. 3–11).

✿ Stick at least 2 more pins through the T2 layer to stabilize it, *anywhere it does NOT overlap the previous layer.* Remove the *center* pin. With tweezers or a long pin, loosen the layer 1 freezer paper template and carefully pull it out. It is no longer needed (Fig. 3–12, page 38).

Fig. 3–10b

Fig. 3–11

Additional Techniques

Fig. 3–12

Fig. 3–13

Fig. 3–14

❀ Now the new layer's freezer paper will guide your stitching. Add a few more pins and baste layer 2 (Fig. 3–13).

❀ Appliqué layer 2 along the solid applique stitching line. Notice how this layer hides some unstitched areas of layer 1 (Fig. 3–14).

8. Continue with layer 3, aligning the T3 petal first.

9. Align the final petal by pinning at the center dot. Then slide the petal halfway between its neighbors. Remove the template from the previous layer. Baste and appliqué only along solid lines, just as previous layers. Keep the freezer paper on for alignment of the flower center circle.

Hint: In case of an error or to conceal accidental misalignment of previous flower layers, an added single petal can be used to cover up. Once the center is stitched on, nobody will ever know if we don't tell them!

10. The flower center circle is the last step. Remember to add a bit of stuffing. Pin through its center, then into the center dot of layer 4 for alignment. Remove the layer 4 template. The circle should cover any remaining raw edges (Figs. 3–15 and 3–16).

Fig. 3–15

Fig. 3–16

Additional Techniques

Fig. 3–17. Block A1 – Dorothy's Double Roses, detail.

Hand Appliqué with Blanket Stitch and Iron-on Fusible

Several floral motifs in the antique quilt are appliquéd with a blanket stitch (Blocks A1, B3, and B4) (Fig. 3–17). The stitches are closely worked to contain the cut edge of the fabric and prevent fraying. Even with the closest stitches I could achieve, sometimes little frays of red kept poking out between stitches. A thin band of iron-on fusible adhesive under the raw edges of the flowers solves that problem. Follow the manufacturer's directions when using fusible; they vary, so read carefully. Stitching covers the fused area and produces a lovely soft edge with no frays and no needle resistance.

Fig. 3–18

Method for Flower A1

The first two inner layers are worked in hand. The last step attaches the outer edge of the flower to the block with blanket stitching (see How to Do the Blanket Stitch on page 43) (Fig. 3–18).

Each flower requires: (Fig. 3–19)

- ❀ 1 square 3½" of a lightweight paper-backed fusible such as HeatnBond® Lite
- ❀ 1 square 2" of yellow fabric
- ❀ 1 square 3½" of red fabric and 1 square 4"
- ❀ Embroidery floss (6-strand): Use single strands of yellow or gold
- ❀ Appliqué needle
- ❀ Sharp-pointed paper scissors
- ❀ Pressing surface (to protect other surfaces from excess fusible)

Fig. 3–19

1. Carefully trace all lines of the flower with a sharp pencil onto the paper side of fusible. Cut the fusible out along the lines indicated in green only, keeping all pieces whole (Figs. 3–20 and 3–21).

2. On the back of the yellow fabric square, place the center fusible section paper-side up and fuse. Cut out the center along the innermost red line, cutting both the yellow fabric and fusible together (Fig. 3–22).

Discard the cut-away yellow square. On the cut-out piece, peel away the thin band of paper revealing the shiny fusible on the back of the yellow fabric. Place the yellow fabric piece face up on the center of the 3½" red fabric square. Fuse (Fig. 3–23).

Blanket stitch all around the edges of the yellow fabric. The fusible band, approximately ⅛" wide, enables a ⅛" stitch width to encase the edge without needle resistance. Now you have the yellow center blanket-stitched onto the small red square (Fig. 3–24).

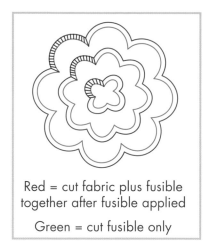

Red = cut fabric plus fusible together after fusible applied

Green = cut fusible only

Fig. 3–20

Fig. 3–21

Discard this piece

Fig. 3–22

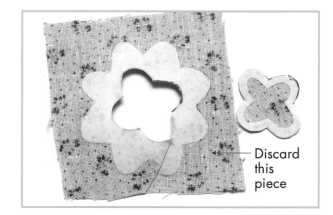

Fig. 3–23

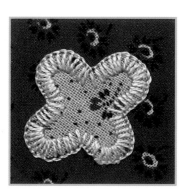

Fig. 3–24

Fig. 3–25

Fig. 3–26

Fig. 3–27

3. Turn the red square (now the flower) over to view the stitching on the back. Center the middle section of fusible, paper side up, onto the back of the flower. Fuse. Cut along the middle red line, cutting fabric and fusible together. Discard the cut-away red square. Peel away the thin band of paper revealing the shiny fusible on the back of the red fabric (Figs. 3–25 and 3–26).

Turn the flower over to view the front. Place the flower onto the center of the larger 4" red fabric square, both face up. Fuse. Blanket stitch around the edges of the inner red flower. Now you have the yellow center blanket-stitched onto the small red square, and the middle red section blanket-stitched onto the large red square (Fig. 3–27).

4. Turn the flower over to view the stitching on the back. Center the outer section of fusible, paper-side up, onto the back of the flower. Fuse. Cut along the outer red line, cutting fabric and fusible together. Discard the cut-away red square. Peel away the thin band of paper to reveal the shiny fusible on the back of the flower (Figs. 3–28 and 3–29).

Fig. 3–28

Fig. 3–29

Arrange the flower onto the block background for permanent placement. Make sure it is correctly placed, and fuse. Blanket stitch around the outer edges of the flower, securing it to the block (Fig. 3–30).

Fig. 3–30. Stitch to block.

How to Do the Blanket Stitch

Use a fine needle, such as an appliqué needle. Separate and cut one strand of floss 12"–18" long. Knot the thread end. To begin the first stitch, bring the needle up from under the background fabric near the edge of the appliqué piece at point (A) without piercing the appliqué (Fig. 3–31). Pull the thread all the way through to secure the knot.

From the top, insert the tip of the needle about ⅛" inside the edge of the appliqué piece at (B) near where the thread emerged from the background. Continue inserting the needle all the way through the background fabric, but do not pull it through just yet. Tilt the needle so that it will emerge from underneath the background just outside the edge of the appliqué piece, right next to the first thread, and OVER the thread loop. I use my left thumb to hold this loop in place.

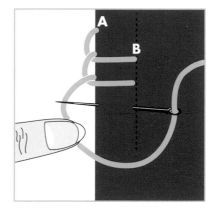

Blanket Stitch

Fig. 3–31

Pull the needle and thread all the way through, just tight enough so that the loop lies along the edge of the appliqué piece. If you pull the stitch too tight, frays might peek out between the stitches. If too loose, the appliqué will not lie flat.

Keep each stitch the same distance apart and the same distance in from the edge.

Each stitch is gradually angled to smoothly cover the edge when rounding curves (Fig. 3–32). At inner points (like the V in a heart) take one extra stitch exactly into the deepest point of the V. At outer points, take one extra stitch exactly at the peak of the point.

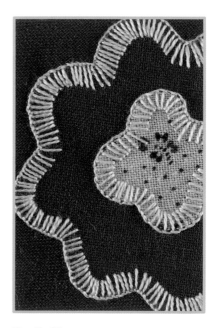

Fig. 3–32

Additional Techniques

Fig. 3–33. Block D1, detail

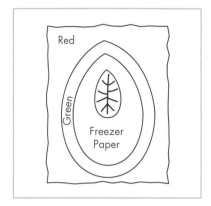

Fig. 3–34

Fig. 3–25

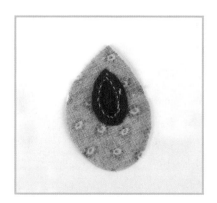

Fig. 3–36

Reverse Appliqué

Reverse appliqué does not mean ripping out stitches! Reverse appliqué is accomplished with the same appliqué stitch, but serves to reveal the fabric underneath. In Block D1, for example, tiny rosebuds are beginning to swell, and a gap is stitched open to reveal a hint of red (Fig. 3–33). Easily stitched in hand, the green calyx opening is first appliquéd to red fabric before being appliquéd onto the block (Fig. 3–34).

First hold the green calyx piece in your hand and make a small clip in the very center of the opening. Cut a scrap of red fabric as large as the green calyx. Baste the calyx onto the red fabric. Working from the top, carefully trim out the center of the green calyx to reveal the red beneath, leaving a tiny green seam allowance (Fig. 3–35).

Clip into the seam allowance at curves and points so that the edges of seam allowance can be turned under. Still working in your hand, appliqué from above with tiny, close stitches all around that opening to reveal the red rosebud beneath.

Turn the calyx over and trim off the excess red fabric, leaving a small red seam allowance. Now the reverse-appliquéd rosebud is ready to be appliquéd to the block (Fig. 3–36).

There are also reverse-appliquéd openings in the ribbon on Block B4 and the vase in D3. Those openings are reverse appliquéd while on the block. Before attaching the piece to the block, remember to cut a small slit to allow those areas to be easily cut open for reverse stitching once the piece is secured.

Taming Tiny Shapes with Cutaway Appliqué

Small appliqué pieces can be difficult to handle. Bird's eyes, for example, can be made with fabric motifs such as a small flower or polka dot. To tame these tiny shapes for appliqué, cut extra-large seam allowances. Place the piece on the block and baste all around on the wide seam allowance. Gradually trim the seam allowance and clip basting stitches out only as much as you need to begin stitching. The first few appliqué stitches will hold the piece in place. Then continue to trim and appliqué.

Fig. 3–37. Block B4, detail.

Olive branches on Block B4 can be handled as one piece (Fig. 3–37). Draw and cut a freezer paper template and press to the fabric front as usual. Cut out the fabric around the template as a large oval. Arrange the piece on the block and thread baste along the freezer paper and on the oval shape. Then cut away some of the oval, leaving a ³⁄₁₆" seam allowance, and begin turning under to appliqué. As the tiny leaves of the olive branch are appliquéd, the branch is secured to the block while the surrounding oval temporarily secures the rest (Fig. 3–38).

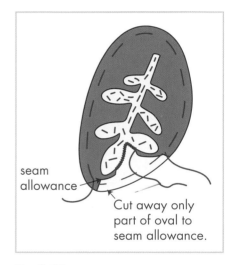

seam allowance

Cut away only part of oval to seam allowance.

Fig. 3–38

Bias Stems

Bias bars made of metal or flexible plastic can be used to make lengths of bias fabric tubes, perfect for graceful curving stems. Make long lengths of bias tubes for stems and cut as much as you need for each block you are making.

Start with strips of fabric cut on the bias (at a 45-degree angle to the selvage) and at least 1" wide. Even for thin bias stems, it is much easier to handle sewing a wider strip and trim seams later.

Fold the strip loosely in half, wrong sides together. Stitch along the fold at the desired width, using a long basting stitch length.

Slip the bias bar inside the stitched fold. Wiggle the seam allowance around the bar so

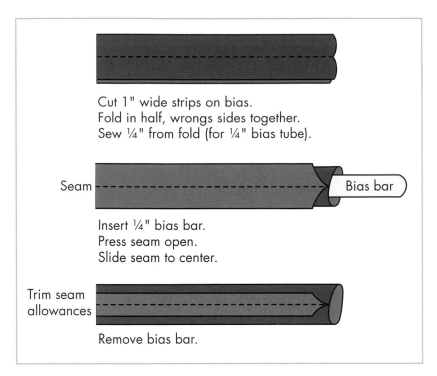

Cut 1" wide strips on bias.
Fold in half, wrongs sides together.
Sew ¼" from fold (for ¼" bias tube).

Seam

Bias bar

Insert ¼" bias bar.
Press seam open.
Slide seam to center.

Trim seam
allowances

Remove bias bar.

Fig. 3–39

that the seam lies in the center of the bar. Finger press the seam open, and with a hot iron, press the seam open along the entire length of fabric. Be careful not to stretch the bias. Remove the bias bar and press again. Trim the seam allowances, one at a time, enough so that none of the seam allowance will show on the front of the stem (Fig. 3–39).

Store bias strips flat until needed, loosely wound on a single layer around a cardboard tube such as an empty paper towel roll. Secure the ends with pins.

Woven Baskets

Make basket weavers with bias bars and fabric strips cut on straight grain (not bias) to prevent bending or stretching. Straight grain is easier to guide into straight lines, especially for weaving over and under.

Fig. 3–40

> *Note:* On the antique quilt, the strips are not woven, but simply laid all in one direction, with all opposing strips on top.

With your pattern underneath the block, draw a line along the center of the basket side, top, and bottom pieces to guide where to cut off weaver strip ends (Fig. 3–40, page 46).

Place all the strips for one direction, pinning them down and through to the foamcore (Fig. 3–41).

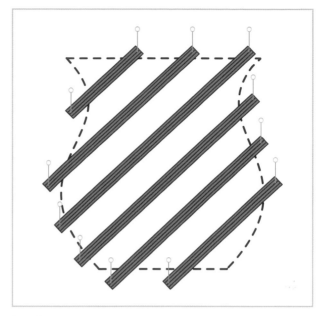

Fig. 3–41

> *Optional:* Use a cardboard box instead of foamcore and push pins all the way down to the ballpoints. Because the pins are mostly out of the way, you can more easily manipulate arranging and basting weavers. The box prevents pins from sticking you.

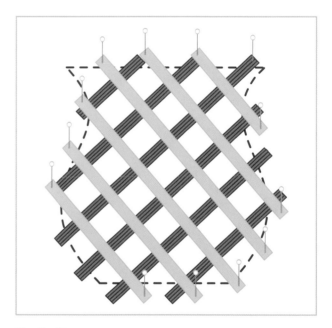

Fig. 3–42

Thread baste all the strips in place, or if you prefer, use a washable fabric glue to baste strips in place. When all the strips are basted in place, appliqué them to the block.

Place all the strips for the opposite direction, pin, baste, and appliqué (Fig. 3–42).

Embroidery Stitches

straight stitch

satin stitch

stem stitch

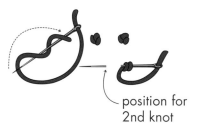

position for
2nd knot

French knot

chain stitch

Optional: If you prefer, weave your basket strips over and under. Pin all the strips for one direction. Avoid pins at intersections. Then arrange strips in the opposite direction, going over and under, and pin to hold in place temporarily. You can still adjust any of the strips and re-pin. Thread baste (or glue baste) the whole woven section and appliqué.

Outer basket pieces made with freezer paper templates cover the weaver strip edges. Before basting those pieces to the background, finger press the seam allowances under, using the freezer paper as a guide. Pre-turning the seam allowances makes it easier to align these motifs over the raw ends of the basket strips.

Embroidery Stitches

These are the embroidery stitches used:

❧ Straight Stitch
❧ Satin Stitch
❧ Stem Stitch
❧ French Knot
❧ Chain Stitch

You can sign and date your work with cross stitching as M.E.C. did in Block C5 or as I did in Block C1. A cross-stitch alphabet is on the CD.

M.E.C. Remembered - Block CI

(Miss Parker's Pompom Dahlias)

Top Assembly, Borders, and Swags

M.E.C. Remembered, Block C2
(Zachary's Zinnias)

M.E.C. Remembered, Block E1
(Natalie's Nasturtiums)

Trim all the blocks to 15½" square, which provides a ¼" seam allowance on all sides. Sew all of the blocks together in rows. Sew the rows together.

Press all seams open to distribute bulk evenly. This becomes critically important when quilted designs float across seam lines, whether quilted by hand or machine. Seams will shadow through to the front evenly, especially if your quilt is hung for display.

Make sure the top section is square—measure across the center (horizontally and vertically) to verify the exact size needed for borders.

Fig. 4–1. Quilt assembly

Mitered vs. Butted Corners

On both the antique quilt and the reproduction quilt, corners are butted together. Top and bottom borders (the width of the quilt block section) are attached first, then side borders (total length of the quilt) are attached. Therefore, instructions for mitered borders are not included.

Cut the background fabric for each border 1"–2" larger than needed to allow for shrinkage during appliqué, fray, or human error. Remember, it is easy to trim later but impossible to make it larger.

Appliqué the borders, swags, and flowers before attaching them to the block section, except the corner swags. When all four borders are attached, then appliqué the corner swags and their flowers.

Back-basting Border Swags by Machine

Try this template-free method suggested by Jeana Kimball for accurate and quick preparation for these long, graceful sweeps of appliqué.

1.   Photocopy 9 swag sections and 2 corner swags. Align all 11 pieces in a row, matching centers and seam lines, and tape them together. Verify that this long paper pattern is straight, and that the length of the border will match the length of the finished quilt top.

2.   From background fabric, cut 2 side borders 10½" x 77" (finished size is approximately 8" x 75"). Cut top and bottom borders 10½" x 97" (finished size is approximately 8" x 91").

3. On each border fabric back edge, lightly mark the center point on each piece. Draw a very light pencil line 1" from the edge to indicate the seam line where the border will join the blocks; this seam line will be trimmed plus ¼" before being joined to the block section.

4. Lay the pattern face up. Lay the border fabric over it face down. Align seam lines and centers.

Note: This border swag design is symmetrical. Asymmetrical designs require a reversed pattern for this method.

5. Secure the layers together with pins, and on the border fabric back, lightly trace the swag design lines as accurately as possible. Do not trace corner swag motifs yet. If adjustments to border size are needed later, corner motifs can be adjusted then.

Hint: To make the pattern easier to see, it is helpful to work on a white surface.

Trace all the side swags onto fabric border backs and remove the pattern; set it aside.

6. Cut 4 yellow and 4 red fabric strips 6" x 76".

7. Lay a yellow strip face down on a light surface. Lay the border fabric face down onto the yellow. Looking through the border fabric, adjust the position of the yellow strip along the inner border swags, following the pencil lines drawn on the border. The yellow fabric strip should overlap all the swag lines evenly.

Top Assembly, Borders, and Swags

Pin the two layers together all along the length to keep them flat and secure, within the swags, above and below. Avoid pinning directly on the lines because you will be sewing along those lines.

8. Working from the back of the border, and beginning at the topmost point of the first yellow swag, machine baste (8 stitches per inch) with white thread along the drawn swag design lines. Take your time and sew as accurately as possible. To manage the bulk, it helps to roll up the border like a scroll, unrolling as needed to feed through the sewing machine. Stitch continuously from one end of the border to the other. Then turn and baste along the bottom of the swag.

> *Optional:* You can do this step by hand using heavy quilting thread and a short running stitch, but I prefer the consistent machine basting stitch for these long swags.

9. Working from the front of the border, trim the yellow fabric along the bottom, leaving the ³⁄₁₆" turn-under allowance for appliqué. Trimming this edge now leaves room for the red strip, to be added next.

10. Follow the same steps for the red swags. Pin and baste.

11. To appliqué the swags, trim away outer fabric from the swags, leaving the ³⁄₁₆" turn-under allowance.

Machine stitching has a top thread and a bottom thread. Clip the first 3–4 top basting stitches and pull them out. The holes in the fabric left behind by the basting stitches will be your visual guide to needle-turn appliqué. As you appliqué, clip and remove just a few more basting stitches only as far ahead as you need to achieve smooth curves.

If you clip every third stitch, you can easily lift and remove them. A piece of rolled up tape nearby is handy to trap the little thread snippets. As you clip and remove top stitches, the bottom thread releases. Hold that bottom thread loosely with your underneath hand to keep it out of the way, and cut it away as needed.

Inner and outer points of swags need not be stitched perfectly; they will be hidden under stems and flowers. After swags are all appliquéd, add the flower motifs to link the swags.

The eight corner flowers must wait for their corner swags until borders are attached to the block section.

12. Join the top and bottom borders to the block section. Add the side borders. Press all seams open.

13. Appliqué the corner swags and the flower motifs that join them across the border seam lines.

M.E.C. Remembered - Block D3

(Margaret's Primrose Vase)

Quilting

 Machine

My reproduction quilt M.E.C. Remembered was masterfully machine quilted by Marty Vint of Dogwood Quilting of Baltimore, Maryland. Bravely, she took on this huge challenge, translating my tracings from the antique quilt, digitizing and quilting those designs with her Gammill® Optimum longarm machine.

After quilting closely around all the appliqués, her job became even more challenging because quilting designs from the antique piece did not always fit on the new quilt the same way. Design interpretations had to be made and a few quilting motifs were added. Marty also agreed to quilt her initials in a vase. (See vase in Block D3, page 55.)

Marty offers this advice:

Selecting your longarm quilter:

❖ Look at their body of work to see if you admire the quilting they have completed. It is essential that they are experienced at quilting appliqué quilts, which must be handled differently than pieced quilts.

❖ Visit their studio. Is it clean and odor free?

❖ In evaluating the quilt top, do they have an understanding of your vision of the quilting for your quilt?

❖ In pricing the work, does the price seem too good to be true? Most longarm quilters are in business, and cannot afford to bargain price heirloom quilting.

❖ Finalize your agreements in writing.

Preparing your quilt top for a longarm quilter:

❖ Carefully press your finished quilt top and lay your top out on a large surface to make certain it lies flat.

❖ Use a lint roller to remove excess threads, hairs, or debris.

❖ For a large appliqué quilt, a high quality, extra-wide backing (instead of a pieced backing) will help ensure consistent quilting. Choose a light color solid or subtle print backing fabric to prevent shadowing through.

✿ Wash and press your backing fabric to preshrink it and remove sizing.

✿ The size of your backing must be 8" longer and wider than your top. This extra fabric is required to attach the quilt back to the longarm frame, and to keep the quilt square. This area is used to adjust tension and stitch quality and allows the sewing head to move all of the way to the edge of the quilt.

✿ Carefully fold your quilt top, placing folds so they do not turn your seams.

Hand

Since M.E.C. REMEMBERED was machine quilted, I did not have to baste the top, batting, and backing, nor did I have to mark the designs for quilting. However, I will offer some ideas for transferring and marking these quilting designs onto your quilt for hand quilting.

Quilted designs on the antique M.E.C. quilt float between the appliqué designs, traveling right across seam lines. Emphasizing these quilted designs, additional quilting is worked in very close rows of diagonal lines across the

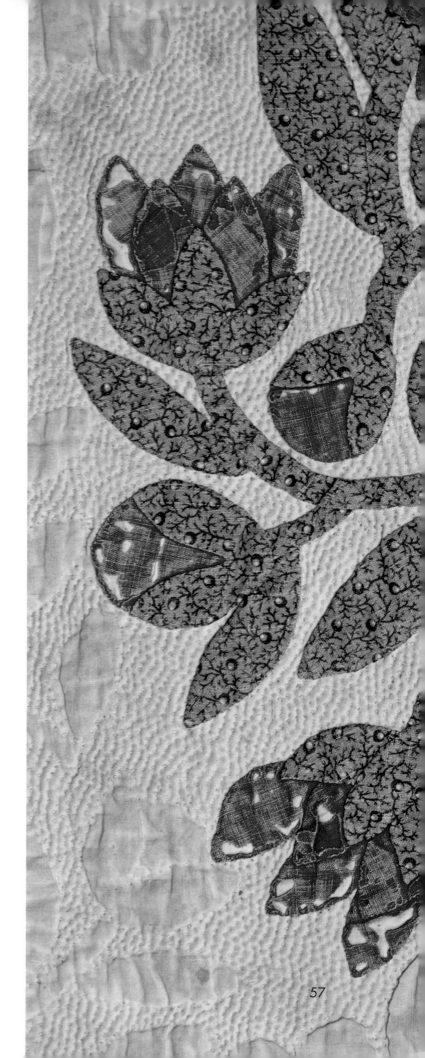

right: Antique M.E.C. quilt, detail.

Barbara M. Burnham ✿ BALTIMORE GARDEN QUILT

Quilting

surface of the quilt. The background quilting lines are so many and so close together that it resembles stippling, at times changing direction to resemble echo quilting. Those lines would not have been marked. Quilting was not stitched around the edge of each appliqué motif, and only rarely stitched on top of the appliqué motifs. (See antique quilt detail, page 57.)

Supplies

- ❀ Marker of your choice. Always test to be sure marks will come out after quilting.
- ❀ Light source or light box
- ❀ Hand quilting needles: I prefer size 12 betweens
- ❀ Hand quilting thread: To match background
- ❀ Thimble
- ❀ Batting: Size of finished quilt plus at least 2" all around
- ❀ Backing fabric: Size of finished quilt plus at least 4"–6" all around
- ❀ Binding fabric: Contrasting color to visually frame your quilt

Adapting & Marking Quilting Motifs

Method 1: Trace quilting motifs onto freezer paper. Cut out the motifs along traced lines. Arrange the motifs on the quilt top. Press lightly with a warm iron, just enough to hold in place temporarily. Draw around the paper with a marker of your choice, cutting away or cutting apart to rearrange motifs to fit the space.

Lengths of bias of any width are flexible enough to form graceful curves for stems. Use found objects such as coins, leaves, and a sketchpad. Cut shapes from template plastic or cardboard for easy repeats. Quilters in the 1850s had to use their imagination and used whatever they had on hand.

Method 2: Place the quilting design pattern under the fabric. Use a light source (such as a light box) and lightly trace designs onto the fabric.

Background Quilting

Background quilting can emphasize the floral designs as seen on the antique quilt. Unless these lines are close together, however, they might distract from the floral quilting.

You might prefer to simply quilt a diagonal grid or straight lines between the appliqués. For marking straight diagonal lines or cross-hatched lines, I like to use a Clover® Hera™ marker to make slight creases on the fabric as a guide. Or, simply place painter's tape to guide the quilting lines. Never leave tape on fabric long term—it could leave glue behind.

Finishing the Quilt by Hand

Use high quality 100% cotton fabric for the backing in a similar color as the quilt top or lighter. Prewash and iron it to remove wrinkles.

Make the backing at least 4"–6" larger than the quilt top on all sides. If you piece the backing, remove all selvages first and press seams open. Seams should be vertical so that the lengthwise grain runs top to bottom (Fig. 5–1).

Plan to add a hanging sleeve to the quilt. Save enough backing to make a matching sleeve. You might not plan to hang this quilt, but you might not always own this quilt. Planning to add the sleeve now will ensure that a future owner will be able to safely hang the quilt, and the sleeve will provide matching fabric if repairs are needed. Reserve a piece of fabric 8½" wide in a length the exact width of the quilt.

Choose a thin cotton batting to echo the feel of an antique quilt and to facilitate tiny quilting stitches.

Lay the backing right side down on a flat surface and secure it with masking tape at several points.

Center the batting over the backing and smooth it out. Center the quilt top over the batting. Smooth it gently and be sure it is parallel to the backing. Trim the batting to 2" larger than the quilt top all around.

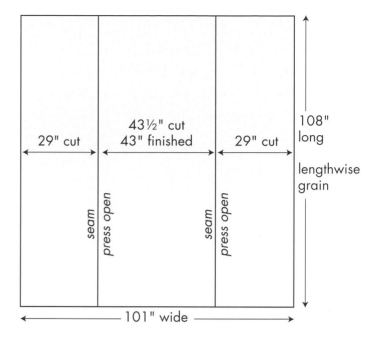

Fig. 5–1

M.E.C. REMEMBERED, Block E2 (Esther's China Asters)

Quilting

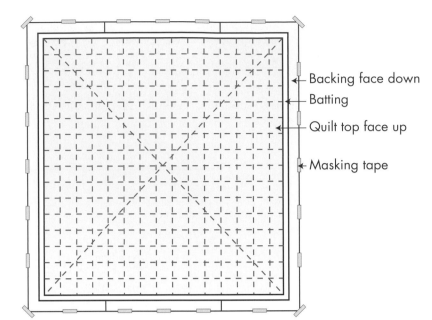

← Backing face down
← Batting
← Quilt top face up

← Masking tape

Fig. 5–2

Hint: Use a large spoon in the other hand to help guide and lift the needle's exit and to avoid pin pricks.

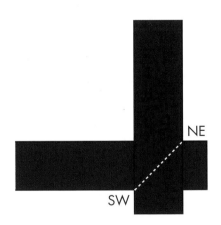

Trim short ends ¼" from stitching line.

Fig. 5–3

Baste the three layers together (backing, batting, and top). Use a long, strong needle and white thread. Starting at the center and working outward, baste all three thicknesses together with large stitches in about a 6" grid, just enough to secure the layers together for quilting (Fig. 5–2).

These basting stitches will be removed when the quilting is completed. Once the quilt is basted, bring the extra backing to the front to temporarily encase the edges and protect the top and batting from fraying during quilting.

Working in a quilt frame or hoop, use a thimble, quilting thread, and betweens needles designed for quilting. They are shorter and stronger than appliqué needles. Work quilting stitches (fine running stitches) to follow the quilting designs. Remove basting stitches when no longer needed.

The antique M.E.C. quilt had a narrow red binding made on straight of grain, although little is left intact. My preference for binding quilts is a French double-fold bias binding.[5]

Be sure the quilt is square. Trim the edges of backing, batting, and top, leaving a ¼" seam allowance through all thicknesses to stitch on the binding. With a walking foot or by hand, run a basting stitch around the edge less than

(5) Dietrich, Mimi, *Happy Endings, Finishing the Edges of Your Quilt,* Martingale & Co Inc; 1987, Revised 2003.

¼" from the edge. This step secures the edges of all three layers, keeps the edges flat, and prevents pleats while you sew on the binding.

Cut bias strips of fabric 2" wide for a French double-fold binding to finish ⅜" wide. Join bias strips to make enough continuous length to go all around the quilt plus 10"–15".

To join bias strips, place strip ends to overlap, right-sides together, at right angles. Sew from northeast (NE) corner to southwest (SW) corner. Trim the short ends to ¼" from the stitching line. Press the seam open (Fig. 5–3, page 60).

Fold the binding in half wrong sides together. Do not press the fold. Leave the first 8"–10" of bias unsewn. Align both raw edges of the binding to the raw edges of the quilt and pin just the first few inches. Machine stitch the binding to the quilt front with a walking foot through all layers ¼" from the edge of the quilt.

1. To miter a binding at the corners, stop stitching ¼" from the corner of the quilt and backstitch. Turn the quilt to sew the next side.

2. Place the unsewn binding up away from the quilt at right angles to the corner. It should form a straight line up and away from the new side.

3. Bring the binding back down along the edge of the quilt, forming a fold along the top, even with the top edge of the quilt. Start stitching at the top edge and continue to sew the binding on, mitering each corner (Figs. 5–4a – c).

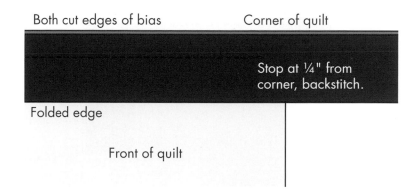

Fig. 5–4a

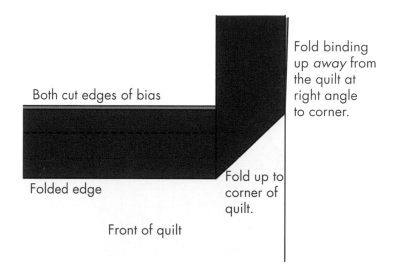

Fig. 5–4b

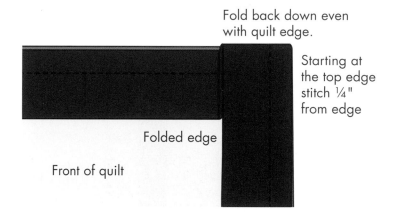

Fig. 5–4c

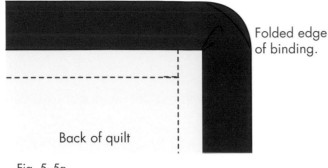

Folded edge
of binding.

Back of quilt

Fig. 5–5a

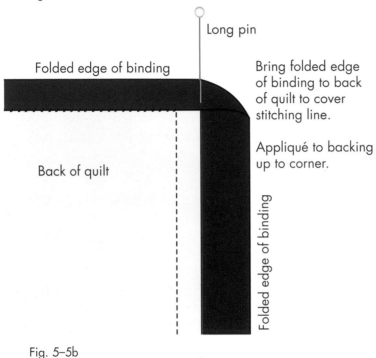

Long pin

Folded edge of binding

Bring folded edge
of binding to back
of quilt to cover
stitching line.

Appliqué to backing
up to corner.

Back of quilt

Folded edge of binding

Fig. 5–5b

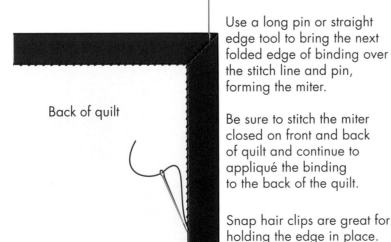

Long pin

Use a long pin or straight
edge tool to bring the next
folded edge of binding over
the stitch line and pin,
forming the miter.

Be sure to stitch the miter
closed on front and back
of quilt and continue to
appliqué the binding
to the back of the quilt.

Back of quilt

Snap hair clips are great for
holding the edge in place.

Fig. 5–5c

Before stitching the last 10", stop. Sew the last joining seam in the binding so it will lie flat; then attach the last few inches of binding to the quilt.

4. To attach the binding to the back, flip the folded edge of the binding away from the quilt.

5. Wrap the binding around to the back of the quilt to encase the raw edges and hide the stitching line. Pin the folded edge of the binding onto the back of the quilt—I like to use snap hair clips instead of pins—and hand appliqué the binding to the backing. Hide knots inside the binding, and check frequently to make sure stitches do not show on front.

At the corners, use a long pin or straight edge tool to keep the fold crisp while you bring the next folded edge of binding over the stitching line, forming a miter. Pin the miter closed.

6. Stitch the miter closed on the front and back of the quilt, and continue to appliqué the binding onto the back of the quilt (Figs. 5–5a – c).

BALTIMORE GARDEN QUILT ❀ *Barbara M. Burnham*

Sign and Date Your Quilt with a Unique Label

Whether an object is a family heirloom, a work of art, or simply a unique object, any trace of identification adds interest and value. This kind of information can provide future generations with a connection to the past, perhaps within their own family. Therefore, the object will more likely be treasured and receive better care. If more of the signatures on this quilt had survived, perhaps this antique quilt would have more to tell us about its history, and it may have lived on in better esteem.

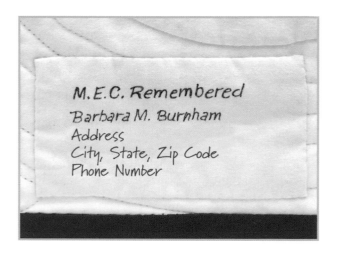

Sadly, in the 1840s when the antique quilt was made, its future value may not have been anticipated. Remember that our quilts often outlive us and our fading memories. Sign and date quilts that you make, and document your treasures for those who inherit them. You might want to cross-stitch your name and date inside a wreath on the quilt front.

Take just a little time to make a documentation label and appliqué it to the back of the quilt. You will have put a lot of yourself and your time into this work. Should the quilt ever become lost or stolen, it will have a better chance of finding its way home.

Happy Stitching!

Patterns on the CD

Important: Before printing the patterns from the CD, open the "index.pdf" file and go to the second page to read about print settings.

Alternate Block Layout

25 Appliqué Blocks (includes quilting designs)

Border Swags

Corner Swags

40 Flower/Leaf Patterns to Join Border Swags

Quilt Motifs for Borders

Cross-stitch Alphabet

Block A1
Dorothy's Double Roses

Block A2
Mary Ann's Mum Garden

Block A3
Amelia's Rose Bush

Patterns on the CD

Block A4
Catherine's Wild Columbine

Block A5
Matilda's Tulip Garden

Block B1
George's Cherry Tree

Block B2
Rachel's Ribbons, Birds &
Berries

Patterns on the CD

Block B3
Calvin's Trumpet Creeper

Block B4
Rebecca's Ribbon Birds of Peace

Block B5
Victor's Honeysuckle Vine

Block CI
Miss Parker's Pompom Dahlias

Block C2
Zachary's Zinnias

Block C3
William's Wild Roses

Block C4
Gertrude's Geraniums

Block C5
Eliza's Strawflowers

Block DI
Polly's Pinwheel Basket

Block D2
Patient Lucy's Basket

Block D3
Margaret's Primrose Vase

Block D4
Jane's Plain Yellow Basket

Block D5
Betsy's Tulip Basket

Block E1
Natalie's Nasturtiums

Block E2
Esther's China Asters

Block E3
Benjamin's Button Mums

Patterns on the CD

Block E4
Peggy's Painted Daisies

Block E5
Parson Timothy's Tulips

M.E.C. 1848 - Block B5

(Victor's Honeysuckle Vine)

M.E.C. Remembered - Block B3

(Calvin's Trumpet Creeper)

About the Author

At the age of five, Barbara Burnham learned to sew from her grandmother, threading a shoestring through perforated cardboard drawings. Embroidery and crewel became her favorite pastimes. In 1972, her mother surprised her with a gift of a year-long Baltimore Album class with Mimi Dietrich. Barbara credits Mimi for inspiring her obsession with appliqué.

When the Baltimore Appliqué Society was founded in 1993, Barbara became a charter member. Very active with BAS, she serves as a board member and frequent contributor to the BAS newsletter, and donates her time and talents for museum fundraisers to raise funds that help preserve their quilt collections.

Barbara teaches hand appliqué, hand quilting, and inking on fabric, and offers presentations and trunk shows at local quilt shows and guilds. She writes articles on appliqué techniques and antique quilts, and is active with online groups of quilt collectors, historians, and appliqué enthusiasts.

Many of her quilts have been exhibited, and she has won awards for hand quilting and hand appliqué in national competitions, including 1st place for Grand Geometrics Created the Amish Way at the American Quilter's Society Show & Contest in Lancaster, Pennsylvania, in 2010. Also in 2010, Barbara and machine quilter Marty Vint of Dogwood Quilting of Baltimore, Maryland, won 2nd place for Bed Quilts: Longarm/Midarm Machine Quilted at the American Quilter's Society Quilt Show in Paducah, Kentucky, with M.E.C. REMEMBERED, the quilt featured in this book.

Barbara and her husband, Ed, live in historic Ellicott City, Maryland, bordering Patapsco State Park. They both enjoy gardening and hosting Eastern Bluebirds in their backyard every summer. Wintertime often finds them both scuba diving in the tropics.

More AQS Books

This is only a small selection of the books available from the American Quilter's Society. AQS books are known worldwide for timely topics, clear writing, beautiful color photos, and accurate illustrations and patterns. The following books are available from your local bookseller, quilt shop, or public library.

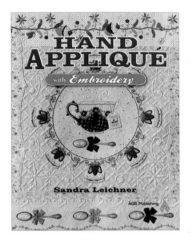

#8244

#8148

#8532

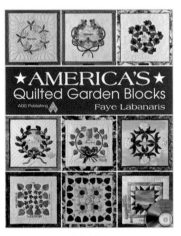

#8530

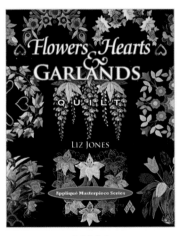

#8356

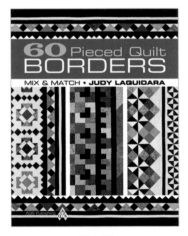

#8662

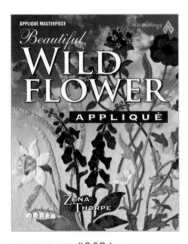

#8526

#8347

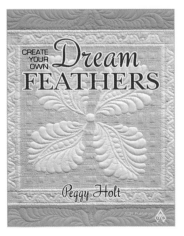

#8670